Microwave
JAMS AND PRESERVES

Text by Judith Ferguson
Photography by Peter Barry
Designed by Philip Clucas
Produced by Ted Smart and David Gibbon

CLB 1658
© 1987 Colour Library Books Ltd., Guildford, Surrey,
England.
Filmsetting by Focus Photoset Ltd., London, England.
Printed and bound in Barcelona, Spain by Cronion, S.A.
All rights reserved.
Published 1987 by Crescent Books, distributed by
Crown Publishers, Inc.
ISBN 0 517 65298 6
h g f e d c b a

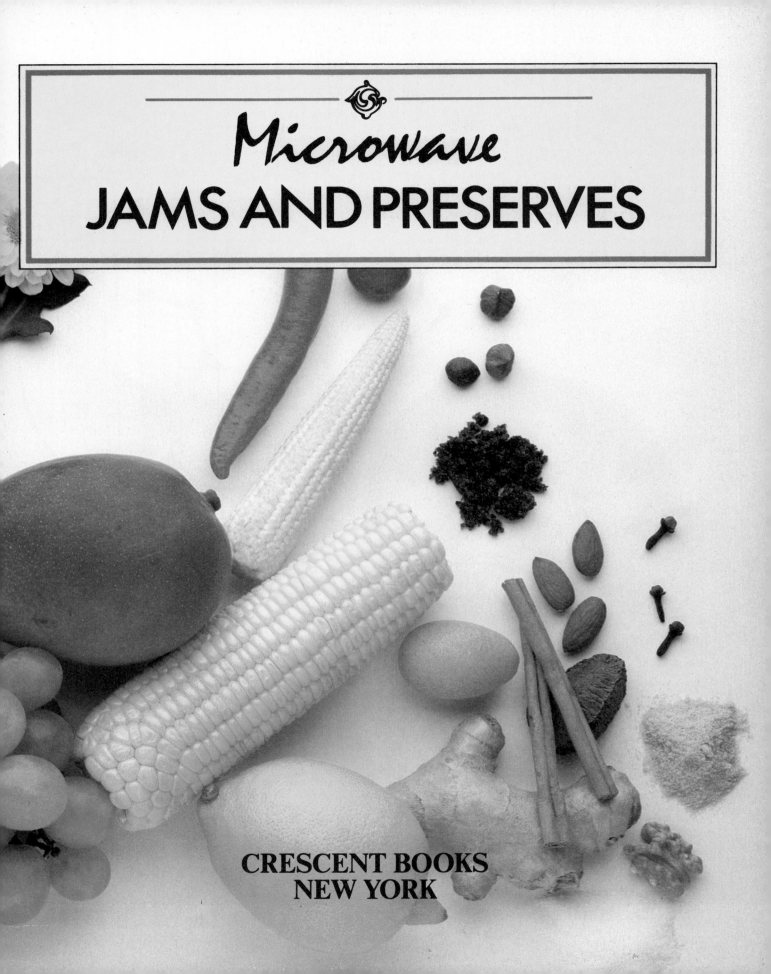

Microwave
JAMS AND PRESERVES

CRESCENT BOOKS
NEW YORK

CONTENTS

Preserving in a microwave oven brings an old-fashioned art up to date, enabling you to make smaller batches of jams, jellies and relishes than would be possible by conventional cooking. Preserves of all kinds are ready in a fraction of the time they take with ordinary methods and without all the stirring and constant attention.

The even distribution of energy in a microwave oven means that the food is heated from all sides, thus avoiding the problem of burned sugar on the bottom of the pan, which can spoil the taste of your preserves and make cleaning difficult.

Perfect jams and preserves can be made in the microwave using equipment as basic as the largest glass bowl that will fit in your oven, and a roll of plastic wrap. The usual type of preserving jar can be used and in the case of jams and jellies any attractive microwave-proof jar will do, with the top sealed with paraffin.

To sterilize jars, simply pour in 1 inch of water and heat for 2-3 minutes on the highest setting. Let the water boil for 1 minute and drain upside down on paper towels. Sterilize non-metallic lids and seals in a bowl of boiling water for 2-3 minutes on high. For long-term storage, jars can be sterilized in the conventional way.

To seal your preserves, follow the instructions for the particular kind of jar you choose. If using paraffin, melt it in the normal way as it is resistant to microwave energy. Pour jam or jelly into sterilized jars and allow it to set slightly.

Carefully pour over a layer of melted paraffin and leave to solidify.

Like all good home-made things, microwave preserves have no additives to prolong their shelf life, and it is wise to store jars in the refrigerator after opening. Pickles, relishes and whole preserved fruit are best stored in the refrigerator as soon as they are bottled. Canning of fresh vegetables should never be attempted in a microwave oven since cooking times and sterilization procedures aren't adequate to prevent food poisoning.

Pectin plays an important role in successful jams and jellies. It is the clear, jelly-like substance found naturally in fruit that makes jams and jellies set. Apples, currants, plums and citrus fruits are high in pectin, while cherries, berries, rhubarb and tropical fruits like papayas are low. Our grandmothers and great grandmothers had to add chopped apple or lemon juice to fruit low in pectin in order to make jams set. Today, however, we can use the bottled or powdered pectin to set jams and jellies – even those made from fruit juice, wine or tea.

All recipes in this book were tested using an oven with a 700 watt maximum setting, although the suggested times should be taken as basic guidelines – experiment with your oven and make your own changes accordingly. Hopefully, these recipes will encourage you to become adventurous: to produce your own creations or adapt old favorites. Even grandma would approve of that!

Microwave
JAMS AND PRESERVES

PRESERVES, JAMS AND SPREADS

Ginger Pear Jam

PREPARATION TIME: 15 minutes

MICROWAVE COOKING TIME: 35-38 minutes

MAKES: Approximately 4 cups

2lbs firm pears
2 cups sugar
¼ cup grated fresh ginger root
1 lemon

Peel and core the pears, and cut them into thick slices. Keep the peels and cores. Peel the lemon and scrape off any white pith remaining on the peel. Squeeze the lemons and mix the juice with the pears in a large bowl. Add the ginger root. Cut the lemon peel into short, thin strips and add to the pears. Tie up the peels and cores of the pears, and the pith and seeds of the lemons in cheesecloth. Put the cheesecloth bag into the bowl with the pears, and cover with pierced plastic wrap. Cook for 15 minutes on HIGH, stirring frequently. Add the sugar and cook uncovered for a further 20 minutes on HIGH or until thickened. Stir frequently. Test by stirring with a wooden spoon. If the spoon leaves a channel, setting point has been reached. If not, cook for a further 2-3 minutes on HIGH. Pour into hot, sterilized jars. Seal and cover.

This page: Ginger Pear Jam (top) and Strawberry and Banana Jam (bottom).
Facing page: Three-Fruit Marmalade (top) and Orange and Grapefruit Marmalade with Whiskey (bottom).

Apple and Calvados Jam

PREPARATION TIME: 15 minutes

MICROWAVE COOKING TIME:
30-33 minutes

MAKES: Approximately 4 cups

2lbs apples
Juice and grated rind of 1 lemon
½ cup water
½ cup Calvados
4 cups sugar

Peel and core the apples and cut lengthwise into thick slices. Put into a large bowl with the water, lemon juice and rind, and cover with pierced plastic wrap. Cook for 15 minutes on HIGH, stirring occasionally. Stir in the sugar. Cook, uncovered, for a further 15 minutes on HIGH. Put a spoonful of the syrup onto a cold plate. If it forms a skin and the syrup wrinkles when the plate is tilted, setting point has been reached. If not, cook for another 2-3 minutes on HIGH. Add the Calvados. Pour into hot, sterilized jars. Seal and cover.

Orange and Grapefruit Marmalade with Whiskey

PREPARATION TIME: 15 minutes

MICROWAVE COOKING TIME:
40-43 minutes, and 30 minutes standing time

MAKES: Approximately 2 cups

2 oranges
2 small grapefruit
2 cups brown sugar
1¾ cups water
¼ cup Bourbon or Scotch
1 tbsp butter (if necessary)

Peel the fruit and scrape some of the white pith off the peel. Cut the peel into shreds and squeeze the juice. Put the remaining pith and seeds into cheesecloth, and tie. Put the juice, peel and cheesecloth bag into a large bowl. Boil the water for 3-4 minutes on HIGH and add ½ cup water to the bowl. Stir the ingredients and leave

for 30 minutes. Add remaining water, cover with pierced plastic wrap, and cook for 20 minutes on HIGH. Uncover, and squeeze the juice from the cheesecloth bag. Stir in the sugar and cook uncovered for another 20 minutes on HIGH, stirring every 5 minutes. The marmalade should boil rapidly. Test by putting a spoonful onto a cold plate. Leave for 2-3 minutes and if a skin forms and the marmalade wrinkles when the plate is tilted, setting point has been reached. If the marmalade is still too liquid, cook for a further 2-3 minutes on HIGH. Stir in the whiskey. If the marmalade is bubbly and cloudy, 1 tbsp butter stirred through the hot mixture will help to clear it. Pour into hot, sterilized jars, seal and cover.

Plum Nuts Jam

PREPARATION TIME: 15-20 minutes

MICROWAVE COOKING TIME:
30-33 minutes

MAKES: Approximately 4 cups

2lbs plums
4 cups sugar
2 tbsps lemon juice
1 cup roasted hazelnuts, chopped

Put the plums into a large bowl with the lemon juice. Cover with pierced platic wrap and cook for 10 minutes on HIGH, stirring occasionally. Leave to cool slightly and remove the stones from the plums. Stir in the sugar and nuts. Cook uncovered for 20 minutes, stirring every 5 minutes. Test the jam by stirring with a wooden spoon. If it leaves a channel, the setting point has been reached. If not, cook for a further 2-3 minutes on HIGH. Pour into hot, sterilized jars. Seal and cover.

Plum Nuts Jam (above right) and Apple and Calvados Jam (far right).

Black Raspberry and Apple Preserves

PREPARATION TIME: 15 minutes

MICROWAVE COOKING TIME: 22-25 minutes plus 30 minutes standing time

MAKES: Approximately 2 cups

1½ cups black raspberries, washed
½lb apples, peeled, cored and chopped
⅓ cup water
2 cups sugar

Put the fruit into a large bowl with the water. Cover the bowl with pierced plastic wrap and cook for 7 minutes on HIGH. Give the jam ½ hour's standing time. Stir in the sugar and cook uncovered for 15 minutes on HIGH. Test the jam by stirring with a wooden spoon. If the spoon leaves a channel, the setting point has been reached. If not, cook for a further 2-3 minutes on HIGH. Pour into hot, sterilized jars. Seal and cover.

Blueberry Jam with Cassis

PREPARATION TIME: 10 minutes

MICROWAVE COOKING TIME: 18-20 minutes

MAKES: Approximately 4 cups

4 cups blueberries
4 tbsps water
¼ cup sugar to every 1 cup fruit juice
2 tbsps lemon juice
⅓ cup pectin
¼ cup crème de cassis (blackcurrant liqueur)

Put the blueberries, lemon juice and water into a large bowl and cook, covered with pierced plastic wrap, for 3 minutes on HIGH. Stir occasionally. Measure the fruit juice and add the sugar. Cook, uncovered, for 10 minutes on HIGH. Stir once after 5 minutes, and add the pectin during the last 2 minutes of cooking time. Test by stirring with a wooden spoon. If the spoon leaves a channel

in the jam, then setting point has been reached. If the jam is still liquid, cook for a further 2 minutes on HIGH. Stir in the cassis and pour into hot, sterilized jars. Seal and cover.

Strawberry and Banana Jam

PREPARATION TIME: 10 minutes

MICROWAVE COOKING TIME: 15-18 minutes

MAKES: Approximately 4 cups

3 cups strawberries, washed and sliced

This page: Black Raspberry and Apple Preserves.
Facing page: Blueberry Jam with Cassis.

3 bananas, peeled and cut into chunks
1 tbsp lemon juice
3 cups sugar
⅓ cup pectin

Put the strawberries and bananas into a large bowl and stir in the lemon juice. Cover the bowl with pierced plastic wrap and cook for 15 minutes on HIGH. Add the sugar and cook uncovered for a further 15 minutes on HIGH, stirring every 3 minutes. Add the pectin during the final 3

minutes. Stir with a wooden spoon, and if the spoon leaves a channel, then setting point has been reached. If the jam is still liquid, cook for a further 2-3 minutes on HIGH. Pour into hot, sterilized jars. Seal and cover.

Lemon Lime Curd

PREPARATION TIME: 10 minutes

MICROWAVE COOKING TIME: 17-19 minutes

MAKES: Approximately 3 cups

Grated rind and juice of 2 lemons
Grated rind and juice of 1 lime
1 cup sugar
⅓ cup sweet butter
3 eggs, beaten

Put the rind and juice into a large bowl with the butter and cook uncovered for 3 minutes on HIGH until the butter melts. Add the sugar and stir in well. Cook for 2 minutes on HIGH. Stir again to help dissolve the sugar and strain on the eggs, Stir well to blend thoroughly. Cook uncovered for 12-14 minutes on LOW, stirring every 2 minutes. Do not allow the mixture to boil. Keep a bowl of iced water on hand in case the mixture curdles. If it does, put it immediately in the iced water to stop the cooking. The curd is cooked when it coats the back of a spoon. Put into dry jars, and cover. Best stored in the refrigerator.

Chocolate, Orange and Hazelnut Spread

PREPARATION TIME: 10 minutes

MICROWAVE COOKING TIME: 8-10 minutes

MAKES: Approximately 1 cup

½ cup unsweetened cocoa
¼ cup butter
¼ cup sugar
Juice and rind of half an orange

1 egg, beaten
1 tbsp evaporated milk
½ cup ground hazelnuts

Put the butter and sugar into a deep bowl and cook for 2 minutes on HIGH. Add the orange rind and juice, cocoa and evaporated milk, and stir well. Strain on the egg and heat well to blend thoroughly. Cook uncovered for 4 minutes on LOW, stirring once. Stir in the hazelnuts and cook for 2 minutes on HIGH. Do not allow to boil rapidly. Have a bowl of iced water ready. If the mixture curdles, put it into the iced water to stop the cooking. Leave to cool, then pour into a dry jar. Store in the refrigerator.

Three-Fruit Marmalade

PREPARATION TIME: 15 minutes

MICROWAVE COOKING TIME: 40-43 minutes, and 30 minutes standing time

MAKES: Approximately 2 cups

2 limes
2 tangerines
2 lemons
2 cups water
2 cups sugar
1 tbsp butter (if necessary)

Peel the fruit and scrape some of the white pith off the peel. Cut the peel into shreds and squeeze the juice. Put the remaining pith and seeds into cheesecloth, and tie. Put the juice, peel and cheesecloth bag into a large bowl. Boil in the water for 3-4 minutes on HIGH. Add ½ cup water to the bowl, stir the ingredients, and leave for half an hour. Add remaining water, cover with pierced plastic wrap and cook for 20 minutes on HIGH. Uncover and squeeze the juice out of the cheesecloth bag. Stir in the sugar and cook uncovered for another 20 minutes on HIGH, stirring every 5 minutes. The marmalade should come to a rapid boil. Test by putting a spoonful onto a cold plate. Leave for 2-3 minutes, and if the marmalade forms a skin

and wrinkles when the plate is tilted, setting point has been reached. If it is still too liquid, cook for a further 2-3 minutes. If it looks bubbly and cloudy, 1 tbsp of butter stirred through the hot mixture will help to clear it. Pour into hot, sterilized jars. Seal and cover.

Rhubarb and Raspberry Jam

PREPARATION TIME: 10 minutes

MICROWAVE COOKING TIME: 13-15 minutes

MAKES: Approximately 4 cups

2 cups rhubarb, cut in small pieces
2 cups red raspberries
4 cups sugar
3 tbsps lemon juice
¼ cup pectin for every 2 cups cooked fruit

Put the rhubarb into a large bowl and cover with pierced plastic wrap. Cook for 2 minutes on HIGH and add the raspberries. Re-cover the bowl and cook for 1 minute on HIGH. Add the sugar and lemon juice, and stir well. Cook uncovered for 10 minutes on HIGH, stirring frequently. Measure the fruit and juice and add the necessary pectin, stirring well to mix. Cook for a further 1 minute on HIGH. Test the jam by stirring with a wooden spoon. If it leaves a channel, the setting point has been reached. If not, cook for a further 2-3 minutes on HIGH. Pour into hot, sterilized jars. Seal and cover.

Facing page: Lemon Lime Curd (top) and Chocolate, Orange and Hazelnut Spread (bottom).

has been reached. If not, cook for a further 2-3 minutes on HIGH. Pour into hot, sterilized jars. Seal and cover.

Apricot Jam

PREPARATION TIME: 10 minutes

MICROWAVE COOKING TIME: 25-28 minutes

MAKES: Approximately 4 cups

4 cups sliced apricots
3½ cups sugar
2 tbsps water
1 tbsp lemon juice
2 whole cloves

Put the apricots, water, lemon juice and cloves into a large bowl. Cook, covered with pierced plastic wrap, for 10 minutes on HIGH, stirring frequently. Remove the cloves and add the sugar, stirring well. Cook for 15 minutes on HIGH, stirring every 5 minutes. Put a spoonful of the jam onto a cold plate. If a skin forms and the jam wrinkles when the plate is tilted, setting point has been reached. If the jam is still liquid, cook for a further 2-3 minutes on HIGH. Pour into hot, sterilized jars. Seal and cover.

Quince and Cardamom Preserves

PREPARATION TIME: 15 minutes

MICROWAVE COOKING TIME: 30-33 minutes

MAKES: Approximately 4 cups

2lbs quinces
1 cup sugar for every 1 cup liquid and fruit
1 cup water
1 orange, sliced thinly
2 tbsps cardamom pods

Peel and slice the quinces. Put the peels, half the sliced orange and

This page: Pineapple and Coconut Jam (top) and Rhubarb and Raspberry Jam (bottom). Facing page: Apricot Jam (top) and Quince and Cardamom Preserves (bottom).

water into a large bowl and cook for 10 minutes on HIGH. Measure the jam, and stir in the sugar. Crush the cardamom pods and add only the seeds to the juice and sugar. Stir in the sliced quinces and the remaining orange slices, and cook uncovered on HIGH for 20 minutes, stirring every 5 minutes. Test the jam by stirring with a wooden spoon. If the spoon leaves a channel, the setting point

Pineapple and Coconut Jam

PREPARATION TIME: 10-15 minutes

MICROWAVE COOKING TIME: 15-18 minutes

MAKES: Approximately 4 cups

4 cups crushed canned pineapple, drained
1 tbsp lemon juice
¼ cup bottled pectin
1 cup shredded coconut, fresh or packaged
2 cups sugar

Put the pineapple into a large bowl. Add the lemon juice and, if using fresh pineapple, ½ cup water. Cover the bowl with pierced plastic wrap and cook for 5 minutes on HIGH.

Add the sugar, pectin and coconut. Cook uncovered for 10 minutes on HIGH. Stir with a wooden spoon, and if the spoon leaves a channel in the jam, then setting point has been reached. If the jam is still liquid, cook for a further 2-3 minutes on HIGH. Pour into hot, sterilized jars. Seal and cover.

Paradise Jam

PREPARATION TIME: 20 minutes

MICROWAVE COOKING TIME:
21-23 minutes

MAKES: Approximately 4 cups

1 large papaya
2 passion fruit
1 guava
1 cup crushed pineapple
2 cups sugar
½ cup water
¼ cup liquid pectin
1 tbsp lime juice

Peel and chop the papaya finely. Cut the passion fruit in half and scoop out the pulp and seeds. Add to the papaya. Peel and chop the guava. Put the fruit, lime juice and water into a large bowl. Cover with pierced plastic wrap and cook for 10 minutes on HIGH, stirring frequently. Stir in the sugar and cook uncovered for another 10 minutes on HIGH. Add the pectin and cook for 1 minute on HIGH. To test the jam, stir with a wooden spoon. If the spoon leaves a channel, the setting point has been reached. If not, cook for 2-3 minutes on HIGH. Pour into hot, sterilized jars. Seal and cover.

Kiwi Fruit and Apple Honey

PREPARATION TIME: 10 minutes

MICROWAVE COOKING TIME:
15-18 minutes

MAKES: Approximately 2 cups

4 kiwi fruit
2 apples, peeled, cored and chopped
1 tsp lemon juice
½ cup water
2 cups sugar
2 cups honey
Green food coloring (optional)

Peel and chop the kiwi fruit. Heat the sugar, honey and water in a large bowl for 5 minutes on HIGH, to melt the

This page: **Paradise Jam.**
Facing page: **Kiwi Fruit and Apple Honey.**

sugar. Add the kiwi fruit, apple and lemon juice, and cook uncovered for 10 minutes on HIGH, stirring frequently until thick and creamy. Cook for an additional 2-3 minutes

on HIGH if necessary. Work in a food processor to make a smooth purée. Add food coloring if desired. Put in hot, sterilized jars. Seal and cover.

Brandy Peach Jam

PREPARATION TIME: 15 minutes

MICROWAVE COOKING TIME: 30-33 minutes

MAKES: Approximately 4 cups

4 cups peaches, peeled and sliced
3 cups sugar
1 tbsp water
1 tbsp lemon juice
Half a cinnamon stick
¼ cup brandy

Put the sugar, water, lemon juice and cinnamon into a large bowl. Cook for 10 minutes on HIGH, stirring frequently. Put the peaches into boiling water for 1-2 minutes to loosen the skin. Cut in half, remove the stones and cut into thick slices. Add the peaches to the hot syrup

This page: Whole Strawberry Preserves with Grand Marnier. Facing page: Brandy Peach Jam (top) and Autumn Jam (bottom).

and cook uncovered for 20 minutes on HIGH, stirring every 5 minutes. Put a spoonful of the syrup onto a cold plate. If a skin forms and the syrup wrinkles when the plate is tilted, setting point has been reached. If the syrup is still liquid, cook for a further 2-3 minutes on HIGH. Add the brandy and pour into hot, sterilized jars. Seal and cover.

Rose Petal and Cherry Preserves

PREPARATION TIME: 15 minutes

MICROWAVE COOKING TIME: 25-27 minutes

MAKES: Approximately 4 cups

4 cups cherries
3½ cups sugar
1 cup rose petals, washed and dried
¼ cup pectin
¼ cup water
¼ tsp rose water

Wash, halve and stone the cherries. Put into a large bowl with the water. Cover with pierced plastic wrap and cook for 5 minutes on HIGH. Add the pectin during the last 5 minutes of cooking time. Stir in the sugar and rose water and cook, uncovered, for a further 20 minutes on HIGH. Test by stirring with a wooden spoon. If the spoon leaves a channel, then setting point has been reached. If not, cook a further 2-3 minutes on HIGH. Stir in the rose petals and pour into hot, sterilized jars. Seal and cover.

Whole Strawberry Preserves with Grand Marnier

PREPARATION TIME: 10 minutes

MICROWAVE COOKING TIME: 15 minutes

MAKES: Approximately 4 cups

4 cups strawberries
4 cups sugar
1 tbsp lemon juice
2 tbsps Grand Marnier

Hull the strawberries, using only firm, unblemished berries. Wash them and leave to dry. Toss the berries and sugar gently in a large bowl and leave until the juice begins to run. Cook uncovered for 5 minutes on HIGH or until the jam comes to a rapid boil. Stir occasionally, add the lemon juice, and continue cooking for 10 more minutes on HIGH, or until the syrup thickens. Put a spoonful of the syrup on a cold plate. Leave for 2-3 minutes. If the syrup forms a skin and the surface wrinkles when the plate is tilted, setting point has been reached. If the syrup is still liquid, cook for a further 2-3 minutes on HIGH. Stir in the Grand Marnier, but do not overstir or the berries will break. Pour into hot, sterilized jars. Seal and cover.

Autumn Jam

PREPARATION TIME: 15 minutes

MICROWAVE COOKING TIME: 35-38 minutes

MAKES: Approximately 4 cups

1 cup apples, peeled, cored and chopped
1 cup pears, peeled, cored and chopped
1 cup plums, stoned and chopped
½ cup water
2 tbsps lemon juice
¾ cup sugar for every 1 cup of cooked fruit

Put the fruit into a large bowl with the water and lemon juice. Cover and cook for 10 minutes on HIGH, stirring occasionally. Measure the fruit, and add an equal amount of sugar. Cook uncovered for 25 minutes on HIGH. Test by stirring with a wooden spoon. If the spoon leaves a channel, setting point has been reached. If not, cook for a further 2-3 minutes on HIGH. Pour into hot, sterilized jars. Seal and cover.

Right: Rose Petal and Cherry Preserves.

Pineapple Grapefruit Marmalade

PREPARATION TIME: 15 minutes

MICROWAVE COOKING TIME:
44-46 minutes and 30 minutes
standing time

MAKES: Approximately 4 cups

1 fresh pineapple

1 grapefruit
2 cups water
1 cup sugar
1 tbsp butter (if necessary)

Peel and cut the pineapple into small pieces. Peel the grapefruit and scrape some of the white pith off the peel. Cut the peel into shreds. Squeeze the juice, and put the remaining pith and seeds into cheesecloth, and tie. Put

This page: Peach Butter with Bourbon (top) and Apple Butter (bottom).
Facing page: Pineapple Grapefruit Marmalade (top) and Plum Butter (bottom).

the juice, peel, cheesecloth bag and pineapple into a large bowl. Boil the water for 3-4 minutes on HIGH. Add ½ cup water to the bowl, stir the ingredients, and leave for 30 minutes.

Add the remaining water, cover with pierced plastic wrap, and cook for 20 minutes on HIGH. Uncover, and squeeze the juice out of the cheesecloth bag. Stir in the sugar. Cook uncovered for another 20 minutes, stirring every 5 minutes. Test by putting a spoonful of the marmalade onto a cold plate. If it forms a skin and wrinkles when the plate is tilted, setting point has been reached. If not, cook for a further 2-3 minutes on HIGH. If the mixture is bubbly and cloudy, 1 tbsp butter stirred through the hot marmalade will help to clear it. Pour into hot, sterilized jars. Seal and cover.

Plum Butter

PREPARATION TIME: 10 minutes

MICROWAVE COOKING TIME: 15-18 minutes

MAKES: Approximately 4 cups

2lbs plums
1 cup sugar
1 tsp ground ginger
¼ cup water

Wash the plums, cut them in half and remove the stones. Put them, with the ginger and water, into a large bowl and cover with pierced plastic wrap. Cook for 10 minutes on HIGH, stirring frequently. Stir in the sugar, and cook uncovered for a further 5-8 minutes on HIGH. Put the contents of the bowl into a food processor and purée until smooth. Strain if necessary. The mixture should be thick and creamy. If it is not thick enough, put back into the bowl and cook for a further 2-3 minutes on HIGH. Pour into hot, sterilized jars. Seal and cover.

Cherry and Almond Preserves

PREPARATION TIME: 20 minutes

MICROWAVE COOKING TIME: 20-28 minutes

MAKES: Approximately 4 cups

4 cups cherries
4 cups sugar
¼ cup bottled pectin
½ cup slivered almonds
½ cup water
¼ tsp almond extract

Wash, stem and stone the cherries. Put them in a large bowl with the water and almonds. Cover with pierced plastic wrap and cook for 5 minutes on HIGH. Stir in the sugar and almond extract, and cook for a further 15-20 minutes, uncovered, on HIGH. Add the pectin during the last 5 minutes of cooking. Test the preserves by stirring with a wooden spoon. If the spoon leaves a channel, then the setting point has been reached. If not, cook for a further 2-3 minutes on HIGH. Pour into hot, sterilized jars. Seal and cover.

Peach Butter with Bourbon

PREPARATION TIME: 15 minutes

MICROWAVE COOKING TIME: 17 minutes

MAKES: Approximately 4 cups

2lbs peaches
1 cup honey
¼ tsp ground cloves
½ tsp ground nutmeg
2 tbsps water
2 tbsps Bourbon

Put the peaches into boiling water for 1-2 minutes to loosen the peel. Cut in half, remove the stones and chop the fruit into small pieces. Combine with all the other ingredients, except the Bourbon, in a large bowl. Cover with pierced plastic wrap and cook for 17 minutes on HIGH, stirring frequently. Add the Bourbon and pour the contents of the bowl into a food processor. Purée until smooth. The mixture should be thick and

Cherry and Almond Preserves (right).

creamy. If it is not thick enough, return to the bowl and cook for another 2-3 minutes on HIGH. Pour into hot, sterilized jars. Seal and cover.

Elderberry Jam

PREPARATION TIME: 10 minutes

MICROWAVE COOKING TIME: 20-28 minutes, and 10 minutes standing time.

MAKES: Approximately 4 cups

4 cups elderberries (substitute raspberries, blackberries, gooseberries or loganberries, if desired)
3 cups sugar
1 apple, peeled, cored and grated
1 tbsp lemon juice

Wash the berries and put into a large bowl. Add the grated apple and lemon juice, and cover with pierced plastic wrap. Cook for 7-8 minutes on HIGH and leave to stand for 10 minutes, covered. Stir in the sugar and cook uncovered for 15-20 minutes on HIGH. Test by stirring with a wooden spoon. If it leaves a channel, the setting point has been reached. If not, cook for a further 2-3 minutes on HIGH. Pour into hot, sterilized jars. Seal and cover.

Grape Jam

PREPARATION TIME: 15 minutes

MICROWAVE COOKING TIME: 21 minutes

MAKES: Approximately 4 cups

4 cups Concord grapes
4 cups sugar
2 tbsps water
2 tbsps lemon juice
¼ cup pectin

Cut the grapes in half and remove the seeds. Put them, the lemon juice and the water into a large bowl. Cover with pierced plastic wrap and cook for 10 minutes on HIGH, stirring frequently. Stir in the sugar and cook uncovered on HIGH for

another 10 minutes. Stir twice while cooking. Add the pectin and cook for 1 minute on HIGH. Pour into hot, sterilized jars. Seal and cover.

Apple Butter

PREPARATION TIME: 10 minutes

MICROWAVE COOKING TIME: 17-18 minutes

MAKES: Approximately 4 cups

2lbs apples
1 cup brown sugar
1 tsp ground cinnamon
4 tbsps water or apple juice

Cut the apples in quarters, but do not peel or remove the stems and cores. Put into a large bowl with the cinnamon and apple juice. Cover with pierced plastic wrap and cook for 10 minutes on HIGH. Push the apple mixture through a strainer to extract all of the pulp. Discard the seeds and cores. Turn the apple mixture into a large bowl and stir in the sugar. Cook for a further 7-8 minutes on HIGH. The mixture should be thick and creamy. Pour into hot, sterilized jars. Seal and cover.

Microwave
JAMS AND PRESERVES

PRESERVED WHOLE FRUIT

Preserved Kumquats

PREPARATION TIME: 15 minutes

MICROWAVE COOKING TIME: 22 minutes

MAKES: Approximately 3 cups

2 cups whole kumquats
2 cups sugar
1½ cups water
2 tbsps Cointreau

Cut a cross in the top of each kumquat. Put the sugar and water into two 2 cup jars and cook uncovered for 4 minutes on HIGH. Put the kumquats into the jars, cover with plastic wrap, and cook for 18 minutes on HIGH or until the kumquats look clear. Remove the plastic wrap and stir in the Cointreau. Seal and cover the jars.

Apples in Ginger Wine

PREPARATION TIME: 15 minutes

MICROWAVE COOKING TIME: 8 minutes

MAKES: Approximately 4 cups

1½lbs apples, peeled, cored and sliced (use a variety that holds its shape when cooked)
¾ cup green ginger wine
¾ cup water
3 cups sugar

Put the sugar, wine and water into two 2 cup preserving jars. Cook uncovered for 4 minutes on HIGH. Put the apples into the jars, cover the jars with plastic wrap, and cook for 2 minutes on HIGH. Reduce the power to MEDIUM and cook for a further 2 minutes. Remove the plastic wrap, seal the jars, and then cover them.

Facing page: Grape Jam (top) and Elderberry Jam (bottom).
This page: Preserved Kumquats (top) and Apples in Ginger Wine (bottom).

Cherries and Peaches in Kirsch

PREPARATION TIME: 20 minutes

MICROWAVE COOKING TIME: 14 minutes

MAKES: Approximately 4 cups

1lb peaches
1¼ cups cherries
½ cup whole blanched almonds
1½ cups water
3 cups sugar
¼ cup kirsch

Put the peaches into boiling water for 1-2 minutes to loosen the skin. Peel, cut the peaches into quarters, and discard the stones. Take the stems off the cherries. Put the water and sugar into two 2 cup jars, and cook uncovered for 4 minutes on HIGH. Add the cherries, peaches and almonds, and cover each jar with plastic wrap. Cook for 5 minutes on HIGH, then reduce the power to MEDIUM and cook for a further 5 minutes. Remove the wrap and stir in the kirsch. Seal and cover the jars.

Brandied Apricots

PREPARATION TIME: 10 minutes

MICROWAVE COOKING TIME: 11 minutes

MAKES: Approximately 4 cups

2lbs apricots
3 cups sugar
1 stick cinnamon
¾ cup brandy
¾ cup water

Put the sugar, brandy and water into two 2 cup jars. Put half the stick of cinnamon into each jar and cook uncovered for 4 minutes on HIGH. Wash the apricots. Put them into the jars and cover with plastic wrap. Cook for 2 minutes on HIGH. Reduce power to MEDIUM and cook for a further 5 minutes. Remove the wrap, and seal and cover the jars.

Spiced Orange Slices

PREPARATION TIME: 10 minutes

MICROWAVE COOKING TIME: 16 minutes

MAKES: Approximately 3 cups

3-4 oranges
1½ cups sugar
1 cup water
1 cup white wine vinegar
1 cinnamon stick
2 whole all-spice berries
4 whole cloves

Slice the oranges into ¼" rounds, discard the ends and remove any seeds. Put the sugar, water, vinegar and whole spices into a bowl or two 2 cup jars. Cook uncovered for 6 minutes on HIGH. Put in the orange slices and cover with plastic wrap. Cook for 10 minutes on MEDIUM or until the orange rind looks clearer. Remove the plastic wrap, seal and cover.

Rum Fruit Compote

PREPARATION TIME: 20 minutes

MICROWAVE COOKING TIME: 20-23 minutes

MAKES: Approximately 4 cups

3 cups mixed fruits (peaches, pears,
cherries, plums, pineapple or apples)
2 cups brown sugar
2 cups water
1 cup dark rum

Peel the apples and pears, cut into quarters and remove the cores. Put the peaches into boiling water for 2-3 seconds to loosen the skin, then cut into quarters and remove the stones. Cut the plums in half and remove the stones. Peel the pineapple, cut it into quarters,

Right: Cherries and Peaches in Kirsch.

remove the core and cut into ½″ thick chunks. Wash the cherries and leave on the stems if desired. Put the sugar and water into a large bowl. Cook uncovered for 5 minutes on HIGH, stirring frequently. If using apples or under-ripe pears, cook them first for 3 minutes on HIGH.

Add all the other prepared fruit and stir well. Cover with pierced plastic wrap and cook for 15 minutes on MEDIUM, stirring carefully so that the fruit does not break up. If the fruit does not look translucent and is still very firm, cook for another 3 minutes on HIGH. Stir in the rum.

This page: Rum Fruit Compote. Facing page: Brandied Apricots (top) and Spiced Orange Slices (bottom).

Pour into hot, sterilized jars. Seal and cover. Keep in a cool place.

Plums in Port

PREPARATION TIME: 15 minutes

MICROWAVE COOKING TIME:
14 minutes

MAKES: Approximately 4 cups

1½lbs plums, halved and stoned
3 cups sugar

1½ cups ruby port
2 whole cloves

Put the sugar and port into two 2
cup jars, and put a clove into each jar.
Cook uncovered for 4 minutes on
HIGH. Put in the plums, cover with
plastic wrap, and cook for 5 minutes
on HIGH. Reduce the power to
MEDIUM and cook for a further 5

This page: **Plums in Port.**
Facing page: **Grapes in Alsace
Wine.**

minutes. Remove the wrap. Seal and
cover the jars.

SWEET AND SAVORY JELLIES

Cook for 10 minutes on HIGH, stirring occasionally. Stir in the pectin and cook uncovered for 1 minute on HIGH, then add the grapes. Pour into hot, sterilized jars, seal and cover.

Apple and Thyme Jelly

PREPARATION TIME: 10 minutes

MICROWAVE COOKING TIME: 20-23 minutes

MAKES: Approximately 2 cups

1½ cups unsweetened clear apple juice
½ cup cider vinegar
2½ cups sugar
⅓ cup pectin
¼ cup fresh thyme leaves
Green food coloring (optional)

Pour the apple juice and vinegar into a large bowl and stir in the sugar. Add the thyme, cover with pierced plastic wrap and cook for 10 minutes on HIGH. Stir in the pectin and cook for a further 10 minutes uncovered on HIGH. The jelly must boil rapidly. Test by putting a spoonful onto a cold plate. Leave for 2-3 minutes, and if a skin forms and the surface of the jelly wrinkles when the plate is tilted, setting point has been reached. If the jelly is still liquid, cook for a further 2-3 minutes on HIGH. Stir in the food coloring. Pour into hot, sterilized jars. Seal and cover.
Note: Other herbs, such as basil, rosemary, marjoram, sage, or a mixture of several different herbs, may be used.

Grapes in Alsace Wine

PREPARATION TIME: 10 minutes

MICROWAVE COOKING TIME: 25 minutes

MAKES: Approximately 2 cups

2 cups white wine, such as Gewürztraminer or Rhine
2½ cups sugar
1 tbsp white wine vinegar
⅓ cup bottled pectin
½ cup seedless green grapes
½ cup purple grapes, halved and seeded
Small bunch tarragon leaves

Pour the wine and vinegar into a large bowl. Stir in the sugar and cover with pierced plastic wrap.

putting a spoonful onto a cold plate. Leave for 2-3 minutes. If a skin forms and the surface of the jelly wrinkles when the plate is tilted, setting point has been reached. If the jelly is still liquid, cook for a further 2-3 minutes on HIGH. Allow to cool slightly, and carefully stir in the flower petals. Pour into hot, sterilized jars. Seal and cover.

Papaya Jelly

PREPARATION TIME: 10 minutes

MICROWAVE COOKING TIME:
25-28 minutes

MAKES: Approximately 2 cups

3 or 4 papayas
1 cup sugar for every 1 cup juice
1 tbsp lemon juice
1 orange
1 cup water
⅓ cup pectin (if necessary)

Wash and cut the papayas into small pieces, discarding the seeds, and put into a large bowl. Squeeze the orange and add the juice and lemon juice to the bowl with the papayas. Put in the orange skins and seeds and water, cover with pierced plastic wrap, and cook for 10 minutes on HIGH. Strain and measure the juice. Stir in the sugar and cook for a further 15 minutes on HIGH, stirring frequently. Test the jelly by putting a spoonful onto a cold plate. Leave for 2-3 minutes, and if the jelly forms a skin and wrinkles when the plate is tilted, setting point has been reached. If the jelly is still liquid, cook for a further 2-3 minutes on HIGH, adding the pectin if necessary for setting. Strain the pour into hot, sterilized jars. Seal and cover.

Chrysanthemum and Green Peppercorn Jelly

PREPARATION TIME: 10 minutes

MICROWAVE COOKING TIME:
20-23 minutes

MAKES: Approximately 3 cups

2 cups unsweetened clear apple juice
1½ cups sugar
⅓ cup pectin
1 tbsp lemon juice

1 tbsp green peppercorns, packed in brine, well drained
1 cup chrysanthemum petals, rinsed and dried (nasturtium or carnation petals may be substituted)

Pour the apple juice into a large bowl and stir in the sugar and lemon juice. Cover with pierced plastic wrap and cook for 10 minutes on HIGH. Stir in the pectin and peppercorns and cook uncovered for 10 minutes on HIGH. The jelly should boil rapidly. Test by

This page: Chrysanthemum and Green Peppercorn Jelly.
Facing page: Apple and Thyme Jelly (top) and Papaya Jelly (bottom).

Port and Cranberry Jelly

PREPARATION TIME: 10 minutes

MICROWAVE COOKING TIME:
15-18 minutes

MAKES: Approximately 3 cups

2 cups ruby port
1 cup whole cranberries, washed

2½ cups sugar
⅓ cup pectin
1 bay leaf
1 tbsp lemon juice

Pour the port into a large bowl with the lemon juice. Stir in the sugar, cover with pierced plastic wrap and cook for 5 minutes on HIGH, stirring once. Uncover, and add the cran-

This page: Port and Cranberry Jelly.
Facing page: Mint and Apple Jelly (top) and Apple Cider Jelly (bottom).

berries, bay leaf and pectin. Cook uncovered for a further 10 minutes or until the cranberries are tender. Test the jelly by putting a spoonful onto a

cold plate. If the jelly forms a skin and wrinkles when the plate is tilted, the setting point has been reached. If the jelly is still liquid, cook for a further 2-3 minutes on HIGH. Pour into hot, sterilized jars. Seal and cover. Store in the refrigerator.

Spiced Tea Jelly

PREPARATION TIME: 10 minutes

MICROWAVE COOKING TIME: 18-19 minutes

MAKES: Approximately 2 cups

2 cups boiling water
4 tbsps loose tea
Rind of 1 orange
1 cinnamon stick
4 whole cloves
1 all-spice berry
2/3 cup pectin
2/3 cup sugar

Boil the water for about 3-4 minutes in a large glass measuring cup. Pare the rind of an orange. Put the tea into a large bowl with the orange rind, spices, sugar and pectin. Cook uncovered for 15 minutes on HIGH. Strain into hot, sterilized jars. Seal and cover.

Apple Cider Jelly

PREPARATION TIME: 10 minutes

MICROWAVE COOKING TIME: 20-23 minutes

MAKES: Approximately 2 cups

2 cups clear apple juice or cider
2 cups sugar
1 tsp lemon juice
1/3 cup bottled pectin
1 cinnamon stick (optional)

Pour the apple juice into a large bowl and stir in the sugar and lemon juice. Add the cinnamon stick (if desired), cover and cook for 10 minutes on HIGH. Remove the cinnamon, stir in the pectin and cook uncovered for 10 minutes on HIGH. The jelly

should boil rapidly. Test by putting a spoonful onto a cold plate. Leave for 2-3 minutes and if a skin forms and the surface of the jelly wrinkles when the plate is tilted, setting point has been reached. If the jelly is still liquid, cook for a further 2-3 minutes on HIGH. Pour into hot, sterilized jars. Seal and cover.

Mint and Apple Jelly

PREPARATION TIME: 10 minutes

MICROWAVE COOKING TIME: 20-25 minutes

MAKES: Approximately 2 cups

2 cups unsweetened clear apple juice
2 cups sugar
1½ tbsps cider vinegar
1/3 cup pectin
1 cup chopped mint leaves
2 cups water

Put the apple juice into a large bowl with the vinegar and water. Cover with pierced plastic wrap and cook for 10 minutes on HIGH. Add the sugar, half the mint leaves, and the pectin, and stir well. Cook uncovered for a further 10 minutes on HIGH. The jelly should boil rapidly. Test by putting a spoonful onto a cold plate. Leave for 2-3 minutes and if a skin forms and the surface of the jelly wrinkles when the plate is tilted, setting point has been reached. If the jelly is still liquid, cook for a further 2-3 minutes on HIGH. Strain and leave to cool slightly. Add the remaining mint and pour into hot, sterilized jars, seal and cover.

Peppered Grapefruit Jelly

PREPARATION TIME: 15 minutes

MICROWAVE COOKING TIME: 45 minutes, and 30 minutes standing time

MAKES: Approximately 2 cups

3 grapefruit
Juice of 1 lemon

1 tbsp crushed black peppercorns
1/3 cup bottled pectin
1/4 cup white rum
1 cup sugar for every 1 cup of juice

Peel the grapefruit and scrape off any white pith. Shred the peel finely and squeeze the juice from the grapefruit and lemon. Put the pith and seeds into cheesecloth and tie it into a bag. Measure the juice and boil an equal amount of water for 3-4 minutes on HIGH. Put the juice, cheesecloth bag, peel and half the water into a large bowl, and leave for 30 minutes to stand. Cover the bowl with pierced plastic wrap and cook for 20 minutes on HIGH. Uncover, remove the cheesecloth bag and press out the juice. Discard the bag. Add the sugar and cook uncovered for 25 minutes on HIGH, stirring frequently. Add the rum and pectin during the last 10 minutes of cooking time. The jelly should boil rapidly. Test by putting a spoonful onto a cold plate. Leave for 2-3 minutes, and if a skin forms and the surface of the jelly wrinkles when the plate is tilted, setting point has been reached. If the jelly is still liquid, cook for a further 2-3 minutes on HIGH. Stir in the peppercorns and pour into hot, sterilized jars. Seal and cover.

Beet and Chive Jelly

PREPARATION TIME: 15 minutes

MICROWAVE COOKING TIME: 17-20 minutes

MAKES: Approximately 2 cups

3 large uncooked beets
½ cup pectin
½ cup distilled white vinegar
1 cup sugar
½ cup chopped chives

Facing page: Spiced Tea Jelly (top) and Peppered Grapefruit Jelly (bottom).

Peel and slice the raw beets. Put into a large bowl and cover with water. Cover with pierced plastic wrap and cook for 7 minutes on HIGH. Drain and mix with the pectin, sugar and vinegar, and re-cover the bowl. Cook for 10 minutes on HIGH or until boiling. To test, put a spoonful of the jelly onto a cold plate. If it forms a skin and wrinkles when the plate is tilted, setting point has been reached. If not, cook for a further 2-3 minutes on HIGH. Stir in the chives and pour into hot, sterilized jars. Seal and cover.

Guava and Lime Jelly

PREPARATION TIME: 10 minutes

MICROWAVE COOKING TIME:
20-23 minutes

MAKES: Approximately 2 cups

2lbs guavas
Sugar
3 limes
2 cups water
½ cup pectin

Wash and cut the guavas into large pieces. Peel the limes and scrape any white pith off the peel. Cut the peel into strips. Squeeze the limes and put the juice with the guavas into a large bowl. Wrap the remains of the limes in a cheesecloth and tie it into a bag. Put the bag into a bowl with the fruit. Add the water and stir the ingredients to mix. Cover the bowl with pierced plastic wrap and cook for 10 minutes on HIGH. Strain, measure the juice, and add 1 cup sugar for every cup of liquid. Add the peel and pectin, and cook uncovered for a further 10 minutes. The jelly should boil rapidly. Test by putting a spoonful onto a cold plate. Leave for 2-3 minutes and if the jelly forms a skin and wrinkles when the plate is tilted, setting point has been reached.

**Guava and Lime Jelly (right) and
Hot Pepper Jelly (far right).**

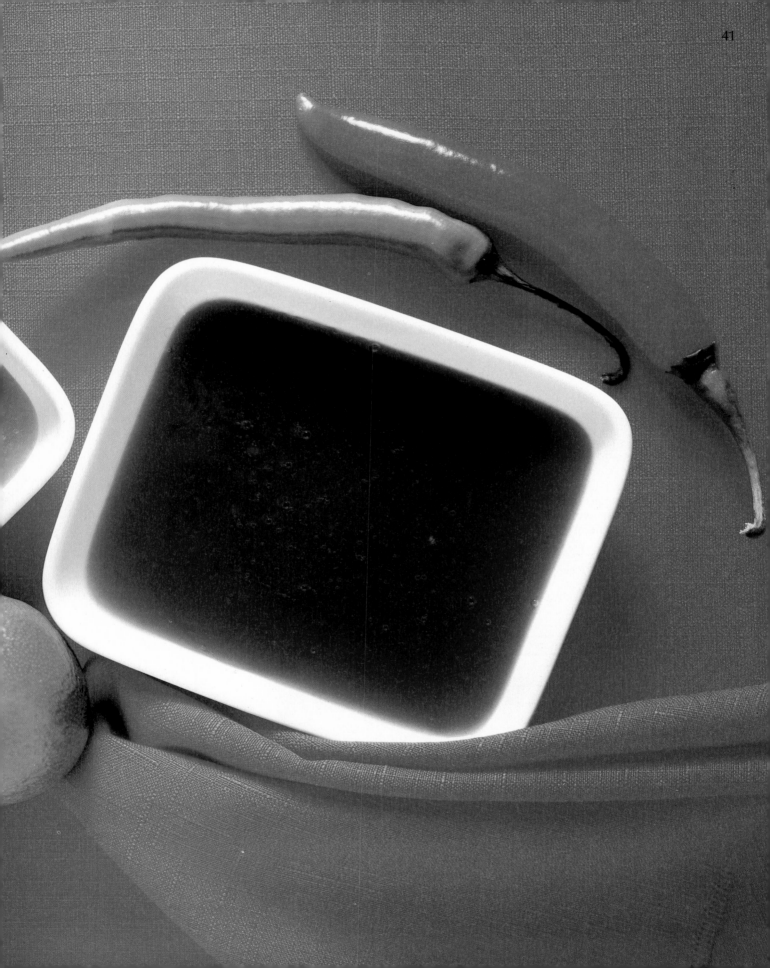

If the jelly is still liquid, cook for a further 2-3 minutes on HIGH. Pour into hot, sterilized jars. Seal and cover.

Strawberry and Pink Champagne Jelly

PREPARATION TIME: 10 minutes

MICROWAVE COOKING TIME: 15 minutes

MAKES: Approximately 3 cups

2 cups pink Champagne, or sparkling wine
1 cup strawberries, halved
2½ cups sugar
⅓ cup pectin

Pour the Champagne into a large bowl. Stir in the sugar and cover and cook on HIGH for 10 minutes. Stir in the pectin and cook uncovered for 5 minutes on HIGH. Carefully stir in the strawberries and pour into hot, sterilized jars. Seal and cover. Jelly is best stored in the refrigerator.

Hot Pepper Jelly

PREPARATION TIME: 10 minutes

MICROWAVE COOKING TIME: 12 minutes

MAKES: Approximately 4 cups

3 sweet red peppers
1 green pepper
2 hot chili peppers
3 cups sugar
1 cup white wine vinegar
¾ cup pectin

Remove the cores and seeds from the peppers. Chop them all finely in a food processor or by hand. Put into a large bowl with the vinegar and cover with pierced plastic wrap. Cook for 2 minutes on HIGH. Stir in the sugar and cook for another 10 minutes, uncovered, on HIGH. Add the pectin during the last 3 minutes of

cooking. Pour into hot, sterilized jars, seal and cover.

This page: Beet and Chive Jelly. Facing page: Strawberry and Pink Champagne Jelly.

Microwave

JAMS AND PRESERVES

CHUTNEY, PICKLES AND RELISHES

Pickled Orange Beets

PREPARATION TIME: 15 minutes

MICROWAVE COOKING TIME:
24 minutes

MAKES: Approximately 2 cups

2 cups sliced beets
Grated rind and juice of 1 orange
½ cup sugar
1 cup distilled white vinegar
1 cup cooking liquid from the beets
¼ tsp ground nutmeg
Salt

Peel and slice the beets and put into a
large bowl with enough water to
cover and add a pinch of salt. Cover
with pierced plastic wrap and cook
for 4 minutes on HIGH. Mix the
orange rind and juice, sugar, vinegar,
nutmeg and 1 cup of the beet cooking
liquid together in a large bowl. Cook
uncovered for 15 minutes on HIGH.
Add the beets and cook for a further
5 minutes uncovered on MEDIUM.
Pour into hot, sterilized jars. Seal and
cover.

Fennel Preserves with Aquavit

PREPARATION TIME: 15 minutes

MICROWAVE COOKING TIME:
20-25 minutes

MAKES: Approximately 4 cups

2-3 bulbs Florentine fennel
1 cup sugar
1 cup distilled white vinegar
1 cup water
1 tbsp caraway seeds

½ cup aquavit
Salt

Cut the root ends off the bulbs and
cut the fennel into ½″ slices. Include
the green tops. Put the sugar, vinegar,
water, caraway seeds and a small

**This page: Pickled Orange Beets.
Facing page: Fennel Preserves
with Aquavit (top) and Pickled
Carrots and Walnuts (bottom).**

pinch of salt into a large bowl or two 2 cup jars. Cook uncovered for 10 minutes on HIGH, stirring frequently. Add the fennel, cover with pierced plastic wrap and cook for 10 minutes on MEDIUM or until the fennel looks translucent. Stir frequently. Stir in the aquavit and pour into sterilized jars. Seal and cover.

Pickled Carrots and Walnuts

PREPARATION TIME: 15 minutes	
MICROWAVE COOKING TIME: 32 minutes	
MAKES: Approximately 4 cups	

2lbs carrots
1 cup cider vinegar
2 cups reserved cooking liquid from the carrots
2 cups sugar
¼ tsp ground nutmeg
¼ tsp ground ginger
2 whole cloves
1 cup walnut halves
Salt

Peel the carrots and chop roughly. Put into a large bowl with water to cover and a good pinch of salt. Cover with pierced plastic wrap and cook for 7 minutes on HIGH. Mix the vinegar, spices, sugar and 2 cups of liquid from the carrots. Cook uncovered for 15 minutes on HIGH. Add carrots and walnuts and cook uncovered for 10 minutes on MEDIUM, or until the carrots look translucent. Pour into hot, sterilized jars. Seal and cover.

Sweet and Sour Onions

PREPARATION TIME: 20 minutes	
MICROWAVE COOKING TIME: 15 minutes	
MAKES: Approximately 4 cups	

4 cups button or pickling onions
1½ cups light brown sugar
2 cups cider vinegar
½ cup water
1 tbsp mustard seed
½ cinnamon stick
Salt

Put all the ingredients except the onions into a large bowl. Cook uncovered for 5 minutes on HIGH, stirring frequently. Remove the cinnamon. Pour boiling water onto the onions to loosen the skins and make them easier to peel. When peeled, put the onions into the bowl with the other ingredients and cook for 10 minutes on HIGH. Pour into hot, sterilized jars. Seal and cover.

Pepper Relish

PREPARATION TIME: 15 minutes	
MICROWAVE COOKING TIME: 15-18 minutes	
MAKES: Approximately 4 cups	

1½ cups sweet red pepper, diced
1½ cups green pepper, diced
1½ cups sweet banana pepper, diced
1 cup onion, diced
Tarragon
Ground cloves
1 tsp celery seed
2 cups distilled white vinegar
1½ cups sugar
Salt
Pepper

Put a pinch of tarragon and ground cloves into a large bowl with all the other ingredients except the peppers, salt and pepper. Cook for 5 minutes on HIGH, stirring frequently. Add the peppers and cook, covered with pierced plastic wrap, for a further 10 minutes on HIGH. Test by putting a spoonful of the syrup onto a cold plate. It should thicken immediately.

Right: Sweet and Sour Onions.

1 cup rice vinegar
4 tbsps sherry
4 tbsps sugar
2 pieces star anise
Salt

Mix the soy sauce, vinegar, sherry, sugar, salt and star anise together in a large bowl. Cook uncovered for 5 minutes on HIGH. If the ears of corn are small, use whole; if large, cut in half lengthwise. Add them to the bowl along with the ginger and chili peppers. Stir well, cover with pierced plastic wrap, and cook for 3 minutes on HIGH. Pour into hot, sterilized jars, cover and seal. Best stored in the refrigerator.

Green Tomato Relish

PREPARATION TIME: 15 minutes

MICROWAVE COOKING TIME: 30 minutes

MAKES: Approximately 4 cups

2½lbs green tomatoes
3 onions, chopped
⅔ cup brown sugar
½ cup dried currants
¼ tsp ground ginger
¼ tsp mustard seed
1 cup cider vinegar
Salt
Pepper

Put the tomatoes into boiling water for 1-2 minutes to loosen the peel, then cut into dice. Put all the ingredients except the sugar, salt and pepper into a large bowl. Cover with pierced plastic wrap and cook for 15 minutes on HIGH. Stir in the sugar, salt and pepper, and cook uncovered for 15 minutes on HIGH, stirring frequently until thickened. Pour into hot, sterilized jars. Seal and cover. Best stored in the refrigerator.

If not, cook for a further 2-3 minutes on HIGH. Season with salt and pepper, and pour into hot, sterilized jars. Seal and cover.

Chinese Corn Pickles

PREPARATION TIME: 8 minutes

MICROWAVE COOKING TIME: 8 minutes

MAKES: Approximately 2 cups

1½ cups baby corn ears
2 red chili peppers, seeds removed and cut into thin strips
1 piece ginger root, peeled and cut into strips
1 tsp soy sauce

This page: Chinese Corn Pickles. Facing page: Green Tomato Relish (top) and Pepper Relish (bottom).

Curried Fruit

PREPARATION TIME: 15 minutes

MICROWAVE COOKING TIME:
15-18 minutes

MAKES: Approximately 4 cups

3 apples, peeled, cored and sliced thickly
6 apricots, stoned and sliced thickly

1 cup pineapple chunks
½ cup raisins
1 cup light brown sugar
½ cup distilled white vinegar
½ cup water
4 whole cloves
2 tbsps mild curry powder
1 tsp coriander seeds

Put all the fruit except the apricots

**This page: Curried Fruits.
Facing page: Apple and Fig
Chutney (top) and Pineapple,
Mango and Mint Chutney
(bottom).**

into a large bowl and toss to mix.
Put the remaining ingredients into a
large glass measuring cup and cook
uncovered for 5 minutes on HIGH.
Pour onto the fruit and mix well.

Cook uncovered for 10 minutes on HIGH, stirring frequently. Add the apricots during the last 3 minutes. If the apples do not look clear, cook for an additional 2-3 minutes on HIGH. Pour into hot, sterilized jars. Seal and cover. After opening, store in the refrigerator.

Chow-Chow (Mustard Pickles)

PREPARATION TIME: 20 minutes

MICROWAVE COOKING TIME: 22-23 minutes

MAKES: Approximately 4 cups

2 cups pickling cucumbers, diced
2 cups onions, chopped
2 cups cauliflower, in small flowerets
2 cups green peppers, diced
1 tbsp yellow mustard
¼ tsp turmeric
½ tsp mustard seed
2 tbsps flour
¼ cup sugar
1 cup white distilled vinegar
¼ tsp thyme
1 bay leaf
¼ tsp salt

Put the first 4 ingredients into a bowl with salt. Cover with water and leave to stand for 30 minutes. Cover with pierced plastic wrap and cook on MEDIUM for 15 minutes. Leave to stand, covered. In a deep bowl, combine the remaining ingredients and beat until smooth. Cover with pierced plastic wrap, and cook for 7-8 minutes on MEDIUM, stirring frequently until thick. Do not allow to boil. Drain the vegetables and mix with the mustard sauce. Heat through for 1 minute on HIGH and remove the bay leaf. Pour into hot, sterilized jars. Seal and cover.

Red and White Radish Preserves

PREPARATION TIME: 15 minutes

MICROWAVE COOKING TIME: 15 minutes

MAKES: Approximately 2 cups

1 cup sliced red radishes
1 cup sliced white (daikon) radishes
1 tbsp grated fresh ginger root
1 tbsp lemon juice
2 cups honey
½ cup Brazil nuts, roughly chopped
2 cups water

Cut the radishes into ¼" thick slices. Put the water into a large bowl and cook for 3-4 minutes on HIGH, or until the water boils. Add the radishes and cook for 1 minute, uncovered. Drain them and mix with the honey, lemon juice, ginger and nuts. Cook uncovered for 10 minutes on HIGH. Pour into hot, sterilized jars. Seal and cover. Best stored in the refrigerator.

Apple and Fig Chutney

PREPARATION TIME: 15 minutes

MICROWAVE COOKING TIME: 30-33 minutes

MAKES: Approximately 2 cups

¾lb apples
1 cup chopped dried or fresh figs
1 cup brown sugar
½ cup chopped onion
¼ cup raisins
1 cup cider vinegar
½ tbsp coriander seeds, crushed lightly
½ tsp ground ginger
¼ tsp Cayenne pepper
Salt

Peel, core and chop the apples roughly. Put all the ingredients except the sugar, salt and Cayenne pepper, into a large bowl. Cover with pierced plastic wrap and cook for 15 minutes on HIGH, stirring frequently. Stir in the sugar, Cayenne pepper, and a pinch of salt. Cook uncovered for a further 15 minutes on HIGH, stirring every 5 minutes, or until thickened. Test by stirring with a wooden spoon. If the spoon leaves a channel, setting point has been reached. If not, cook for a further 2-3 minutes on HIGH.

Pour into hot, sterilized jars, seal and cover.

Pineapple, Mango and Mint Chutney

PREPARATION TIME: 20 minutes

MICROWAVE COOKING TIME: 30-35 minutes

MAKES: Approximately 4 cups

3 cups fresh pineapple, chopped
1 large mango, peeled and chopped
1 cup sugar
2 cups distilled white vinegar
1 cup white raisins
2 tbsps chopped fresh mint
¼ tsp ground nutmeg
1 small piece ginger root
Salt

Sprinkle the pineapple with a good pinch of salt and leave for half an hour. Peel the ginger root and cut into thin slivers. Drain the pineapple and rinse in cold water. Put all the ingredients except the sugar into a large bowl. Cover with pierced plastic wrap and cook for 15 minutes on HIGH, stirring frequently. Add the sugar and cook uncovered for a further 15 minutes on HIGH or until thickened. Stir frequently. Test by stirring with a wooden spoon. If the spoon leaves a channel, then setting point has been reached. If not, cook for a further 5 minutes on HIGH. Add another pinch of salt if necessary and pour into hot, sterilized jars. Seal and cover.

Facing Page: Red and White Radish Preserves (top) and Chow-Chow (Mustard Pickles) (bottom).

55

Bread and Butter Pickles

PREPARATION TIME: 10 minutes

MICROWAVE COOKING TIME:
11 minutes

MAKES: Approximately 4 cups

4 cups pickling cucumbers, sliced to ¼"
* thick*
2 cups distilled white vinegar
2 cups sugar
¼ tsp turmeric
2 tbsps mustard seed
Cayenne pepper
¼ tsp alum
1 tbsp water
Salt

Mix the cucumbers with the salt, alum and water, and leave for 1 hour. Rinse well under cold water and dry. Sterilize two 2 cup jars and divide all the ingredients except the cucumbers between them, adding a good pinch of Cayenne pepper. Stir well and cook uncovered for 8 minutes on HIGH. Add the cucumbers, cover with plastic wrap and cook for a further 3 minutes on MEDIUM. Do not let the cucumbers boil in the liquid. Seal and cover the jars.

Tarragon Vinegar Pickles

PREPARATION TIME: 15 minutes

MICROWAVE COOKING TIME:
13 minutes

MAKES: Approximately 4 cups

4 cups whole small pickling cucumbers
1 cup sugar
1½ cups white wine vinegar
½ cup water
1 large bunch tarragon
Black peppercorns
¼ tsp alum
1 tbsp water
Salt

If the cucumbers are small, leave them whole; if not, cut them into quarters lengthwise. Salt them, mix with the alum and water, and leave for 1 hour. Rinse under cold water and dry. Put the sugar, vinegar, water,

Pumpkin Chutney

PREPARATION TIME: 20 minutes

MICROWAVE COOKING TIME:
45-48 minutes

MAKES: Approximately 4 cups

4 cups pumpkin, peeled and cubed
2 cups light brown sugar
1 lemon, thinly sliced
1 tbsp grated ginger root
1¼ cups water
1 cup cider vinegar
1 cup raisins

Put the pumpkin, lemon slices, ginger root, raisins, water and vinegar into a

This page: Pumpkin Chutney. Facing page: Bread and Butter Pickles (top) and Tarragon Vinegar Pickles (bottom).

large bowl. Cover with pierced plastic wrap and cook for 15 minutes on HIGH, stirring frequently. Stir in the sugar thoroughly and cook uncovered for a further 20 minutes on HIGH, or until thickened. Test by stirring with a wooden spoon. If the spoon leaves a channel, setting point has been reached. If not, cook a further 2-3 minutes on HIGH. Pour into hot, sterilized jars, seal and cover.

tarragon and peppercorns into a bowl, or two 2 cup jars. Cook uncovered for 10 minutes on HIGH. Put in the cucumbers, cover with plastic wrap and cook on MEDIUM for 3 minutes or until the cucumbers lose their bright green color. Seal and cover the jars.

Watermelon and Lime Pickles

PREPARATION TIME: 20 minutes plus overnight standing

MICROWAVE COOKING TIME: 25 minutes

MAKES: Approximately 4 cups

4 cups watermelon rind, cut into cubes
3 limes
1 cup distilled white vinegar
½ cup lime juice
1½ cups sugar
1 stick cinnamon
2 whole cloves
½ tsp powdered alum
Salt

Save the rinds from a watermelon and peel off the dark green skin. Scrape off any remaining flesh and cut the rind into 1″ cubes. Mix the alum together with a pinch of salt and the cold water. Pour over the rind and add more water to cover. Leave to stand overnight. Rinse under cold water and drain. Slice 2 limes into thin rounds and squeeze the juice from the third lime. Combine the juice, vinegar, spices and sugar in a large bowl and cook uncovered for 10 minutes on HIGH. Remove the spices and add the prepared watermelon rind. Cook uncovered for 15 minutes on MEDIUM, or until the rind looks translucent. Stir occasionally. Add the lime slices during the last 3 minutes. Pour into hot, sterilized jars. Seal and cover.

Spicy Cantaloupe Pickles

PREPARATION TIME: 15 minutes

MICROWAVE COOKING TIME: 15 minutes, plus 2 hours soaking time

MAKES: Approximately 4 cups

2 cantaloupe melons, slightly under-ripe
1½ cups sugar
1½ cups distilled white vinegar
½ cup water
4 whole cloves
1 stick cinnamon

Cut the melons in half and remove the seeds. Cut the melons into quarters and remove the rind. Cut the flesh into 1″ chunks. Mix the sugar, spices, water and vinegar together in a large bowl and cook uncovered on HIGH for 10 minutes. Put in the cantaloupe and leave to soak in the syrup for 2 hours. After the melon has soaked up some of the syrup, cook for a further 5 minutes on HIGH or just until the syrup

**This page: Corn Relish.
Facing page: Watermelon and Lime Pickles (top) and Spicy Cantaloupe Pickles (bottom).**

comes to the boil. Pour into sterilized jars, seal and cover. Once the jars have been opened, store the pickles in the refrigerator.

Corn Relish

PREPARATION TIME: 15 minutes

MICROWAVE COOKING TIME:
20-23 minutes

MAKES: Approximately 4 cups

2 cups frozen or fresh corn
2 red peppers, diced
1 cup chopped celery
1 onion, chopped
½ cup sugar
1¼ cups distilled white vinegar
1 tbsp cornstarch
¾ cup water
½ tbsp celery seed
1 tsp mustard seed
¼ tsp turmeric
Salt
Pepper

Put all the ingredients except the corn, sugar, salt and pepper into a large bowl and stir well to mix in the cornstarch. Cover with pierced plastic wrap and cook on HIGH for 5 minutes, stirring occasionally. Add the corn, sugar, salt and pepper, mixing thoroughly. Cover and cook for a further 15-18 minutes on HIGH, stirring frequently until thickened.

Chili Sauce

PREPARATION TIME: 15 minutes

MICROWAVE COOKING TIME:
30 minutes

MAKES: Approximately 4 cups

1½lbs tomatoes, peeled and diced
3 large onions, chopped
2 green peppers, diced
⅔ cup brown sugar
1 cup cider vinegar
¼ tsp ground cloves
¼ tsp ground cinnamon
1 tsp mustard seed
1 tsp celery seed
½ tsp chili powder
Pinch ground all-spice
1 bay leaf
Salt
Pepper

Put all the ingredients except the

sugar, salt and pepper into a large bowl. Cover with pierced plastic wrap, and cook for 15 minutes on HIGH. Stir in the sugar, salt and pepper, and cook uncovered for a further 15 minutes on HIGH or until the mixture thickens. Remove the bay leaf, and pour into hot, sterilized jars. Seal and cover. Best stored in the refrigerator.

Cranberry Orange Relish

PREPARATION TIME: 15 minutes

MICROWAVE COOKING TIME:
11 minutes

This page: **Cranberry Orange Relish.**
Facing page: **Chili Sauce (top) and Mock Mincemeat (bottom).**

MAKES: Approximately 4 cups

5 cups whole cranberries
3 small oranges
¼ cup sugar
¾ cup red wine
½ tsp ground all-spice
1 tbsp red wine vinegar (optional)

Squeeze the juice from the oranges. Scrape the white pith from the peel

1½ tbsps ground mustard
2 tsps mustard seed
Salt

Put the sugar, mustard powder and seed, water, vinegar and a pinch of salt into a large bowl and mix the ingredients together thoroughly. Cook on HIGH, uncovered, for 4 minutes. Add all the fruit and stir well. Leave to stand covered for 30 minutes. Cook uncovered for 10 minutes on HIGH. Pour into hot, sterilized jars. Seal and cover. After opening, store in the refrigerator.

Mock Mincemeat

PREPARATION TIME: 15 minutes

MICROWAVE COOKING TIME: 22 minutes

MAKES: Approximately 4 cups

2lbs apples, peeled, cored and chopped
1¾ cups seedless raisins
½ cup candied peel, chopped
½ cup dark brown sugar
½ tsp nutmeg
2 tsps cinnamon
½ tsp ground cloves
¼ tsp ground ginger
¾ cup water
Grated rind and juice of 1 orange
¼ cup rum

Put all the ingredients except the rum and sugar into a large bowl. Cover with pierced plastic wrap and cook for 15 minutes on HIGH. Add the sugar and cook a further 2 minutes, uncovered, on HIGH. Put into hot, sterilized jars and fill to within 1″ of the top. Cover each jar with plastic wrap and cook for a further 5 minutes on HIGH. Remove the wrap and stir in the rum. Seal and cover the jars.

and chop the peel in a food processor. Wash the cranberries, add them to the food processor and chop roughly. Put the sugar, orange juice and all-spice into a large bowl and cook uncovered for 4 minutes on HIGH. Add the cranberries, orange rind and wine, and cook for 5 minutes on HIGH, stirring frequently. Cook until the rind and cranberries are just tender. Taste, add the red wine vinegar if the mixture is too sweet, and continue to cook for 2-3 minutes on HIGH. Pour into hot, sterilized jars. Seal and cover Best kept in the refrigerator.

Mustard Fruit

PREPARATION TIME: 15 minutes

MICROWAVE COOKING TIME: 14 minutes, plus 30 minutes standing time

MAKES: Approximately 4 cups

1½ cups dried fruit (prunes, apricots, peaches, pears, apples, figs), left whole
1½ cups candied fruit (cherries, citron peel, pineapple slices or pieces), left whole
1½ cups sugar
2½ cups water
½ cup white wine vinegar

**This page: Mustard Fruit.
Facing page: Lemon Vinegar (top) and Garlic Vinegar (bottom).**

FLAVORED SYRUPS AND VINEGARS

Garlic Vinegar

PREPARATION TIME: 5 minutes

MICROWAVE COOKING TIME:
1½ minutes

MAKES: Approximately 2 cups

2 cups cider vinegar
3 cloves garlic, peeled
1 bay leaf

Thread the cloves of garlic onto a wooden skewer. Put this into a 2 cup bottle of cider vinegar, along with the bay leaf. Cook for 1½ minutes on HIGH or until the bottle is warm. Check after 30 seconds to make sure that the bottle is not overheating. Cover while still warm and store in a cool, dark place for 2 weeks before using. Keeps 2 months.

Raspberry Syrup

PREPARATION TIME: 5 minutes

MICROWAVE COOKING TIME:
10 minutes

MAKES: 4 cups

5 cups red raspberries, fresh or frozen
1½ cups sugar
¾ cup water
¼ cup raspberry liqueur (optional)
Half a cinnamon stick
1 tbsp lemon juice

Wash the raspberries and put into a large bowl with the water and the cinnamon. Cover with pierced plastic wrap and cook for 3 minutes on HIGH or until the berries break up. Strain and mix with the sugar.

Remove the cinnamon and return the liquid to the bowl. Cook uncovered for 7 minutes on HIGH. Add the raspberry liqueur (if desired), and lemon juice to taste.

Pour into bottles or jars, and cover. Keep in a refrigerator. Drink mixed with 2 parts soda water or dry white wine to 1 part syrup, or use with desserts.

Cherry Vinegar

PREPARATION TIME: 5 minutes

MICROWAVE COOKING TIME:
1½ minutes

MAKES: Approximately 2 cups

½ cup red or black cherries, stems left on
1 cup distilled white vinegar
Pinch sugar

Put all the ingredients into a bowl and cook, covered, for 1½ minutes on HIGH. Check after 30 seconds to ensure the mixture is not over-heating. If the cherries do not color the vinegar, crush them slightly and heat for 30 seconds more on HIGH. Pour into bottles and seal while still warm. Store in a cool place for 2 weeks before using.
Keeps 2 months.

Lemon Vinegar

PREPARATION TIME: 5 minutes

MICROWAVE COOKING TIME:
1½ minutes

MAKES: Approximately 1 cup

1 cup distilled white vinegar
Juice and rind of 1 lemon
½ tsp sugar

Pour the lemon juice and vinegar together into a bottle. Add the sugar and cook for 1½ minutes on HIGH or until the bottle is just warm to the touch. Check the bottle after 30 seconds to make sure it is not over-heating. Shred the lemon rind finely and push into the bottle. Cover the bottle while still warm, and store in a cool, dark place for 2 weeks before using. Keeps 2 months.

Blueberry Syrup

PREPARATION TIME: 5 minutes

MICROWAVE COOKING TIME:
10 minutes

MAKES: Approximately 4 cups

4 cups blueberries, fresh or frozen
1 cup sugar
½ cup water
¼ cup crème de cassis (optional)
1 tbsp lemon juice

Wash the blueberries, and put into a large bowl with the water. Cover with pierced plastic wrap and cook for 3 minutes on HIGH, or until the berries break up. Strain and mix with the sugar. Return to the bowl and cook uncovered for 7 minutes on HIGH. Stir in the cassis (if desired), and lemon juice to taste. Pour into bottles or jars, and cover. Keep in a refrigerator. Drink mixed with 2 parts soda or dry white wine to 1 part syrup, or use with desserts.

Rosemary Vinegar

PREPARATION TIME: 5 minutes

MICROWAVE COOKING TIME:
1 minute

MAKES: Approximately 1 cup

1 cup red wine vinegar
6 sprigs fresh rosemary
3 black peppercorns

Put the rosemary into a bottle with the red wine vinegar. Add the peppercorns and cook for 30 seconds to 1 minute on HIGH until the bottle is warm to the touch. After 15 seconds, check the temperature of the bottle to make sure it is not over-heating. Cover while still warm and keep in a cool, dark place for 2 weeks before using. Keeps about 2 months.

This page: Blueberry Syrup (top)
and Raspberry Syrup (bottom).
Facing page: Cherry Vinegar (top)
and Rosemary Vinegar (bottom).

Microwave
JAMS AND PRESERVES

INDEX